The Missions of California

Mission San Gabriel Arcángel

Alice B. McGinty

The Rosen Publishing Group's
PowerKids Press™
New York

Published in 2000 by The Rosen Publishing Group, Inc.
29 East 21st Street, New York, NY 10010

Photo Credits and Photo Illustrations: pp.1, 4, 28, 29, 32, 34 (all), 35, 46, 47, 49, 50 by Cristina Taccone; p. 5 © The Bridgeman Art Library International Ltd, New York; pp. 7, 45 © The Granger Collection, New York; p. 8 © CORBIS/Baldwin H. Ward; p. 11 © The Huntington Library, Art Collections, and Botanical Gardens, San Marino, California/Superstock; pp. 12, 39 by Tim Hall; p. 15 © Seaver Center for Western History Research, LA County Museum of Natural History; pp. 19, 48 © CORBIS/Arte & Immagini srl; p. 20 © Eremitani Chapel, Padua, Italy/Mauro Magliani/Superstock; p. 23 © CORBIS/Bettman; p. 24 © David David Gallery, Philadelphia/Superstock; p.26 © CORBIS/Craig Lovell; p. 26 © CORBIS/Richard Cummins; p. 28 © CORBIS/Philippa Lewis; Edifice; pp. 29, 31 by Eda Rogers; pp. 32, 41, 50, 51 by Shirley Jordan; p. 37 © Christie's Images/Superstock; p. 43 © Rieger Communications; pp. 52, 57 by Christine Innamorato.

First Edition

Book Design: Danielle Primiceri

Layout: Kim Sonsky

Editorial Consultant Coordinator: Karen Fontanetta, M.A., Curator, Mission San Miguel Arcángel
Editorial Consultant: Thomas L. Davis, M.Div, M.A.
Historical Photo Consultants: Thomas L. Davis, M.Div., M.A.
                              Michael K. Ward, M.A.

McGinty, Alice B.
    Mission San Gabriel Arcángel / by Alice B. McGinty.
       p.   cm. — (The missions of California)
    Includes bibliographical references and index.
    Summary: Discusses the founding, building, operation and closing of the Spanish mission at San Gabriel and its role in California history.
    ISBN 0-8239-5490-0 (lib.bdg. : alk. paper)
    1. Mission San Gabriel Arcángel (San Gabriel, Calif.)—History—Juvenile literature. 2. Spanish mission buildings—California—San Gabriel Region—History—Juvenile literature. 3. Franciscans—California—San Gabriel Region—History—Juvenile literature. 4. California—History—To 1846—Juvenile literature. 5. Chumash Indians—Missions—California—San Gabriel Region—History—Juvenile literature. [1. Mission San Gabriel Arcángel (San Gabriel, Calif.)—History. 2. Missions—California. 3. Indians of North America—California—Missions.] I. Title. II. Series.
F869.M655M34   1999
979.4'93—DC21
                         99-19097
                         CIP

Contents

The Spaniards Arrive in Alta California

Surrounded by the city of Los Angeles, in busy downtown San Gabriel, there stands a large church. This fortress-like building may look a bit out of place in modern California, but it is impossible to know its amazing story at first glance. Mission San Gabriel's story tells of struggle, accomplishment, a clash between cultures, and bitter defeat. To understand Mission San Gabriel Arcángel is to understand California.

Spanish Exploration

The story of California's missions began in the 1760s. King Carlos III of Spain had a problem. His Spanish ships needed places to dock along the west coast of North America. The king wanted Spain to ensure his claim on the land they called Alta, or upper, California, before Russian or English people settled there.

The country of Spain had claimed many new lands in search of power and gold. With a small group of Spaniards and some supplies, Spain established missions in the new land. Spanish missions were like small towns governed by friars. The American Indians in the new land joined the missions, worked there, and learned the friars' religion, Catholicism. The plan was that the missions would later be turned into *pueblos*, or Spanish towns, and the American Indians would live there as Spanish citizens. Spain had already

▲

King Carlos III wanted to claim land in California.

◀ *Today, Mission San Gabriel is a reminder of California's history.*

5

used the mission system to take over land in New Spain (Mexico), Florida, Texas, and Baja, or lower, California.

In 1768, King Carlos III told the viceroy in New Spain to start settling the northern frontier of New Spain. A viceroy was the person chosen to rule for the king in a new land. The king sent his officer, Inspector General Jose de Galvez, to help. Soon a group of missionaries and soldiers were ready to carry out the king's plan.

The California Missions

The leader of the missionaries was a Franciscan friar named Fray Junípero Serra. He and the other friars were called missionaries because they were on a

San Francisco de Solano
San Rafael Arcángel
San Francisco de Asís
San José
Santa Clara de Asís
Santa Cruz
San Juan Bautista
San Carlos Borromeo del Río Carmelo
Nuestra Señora de la Soledad
San Antonio de Padua
San Miguel Arcángel
San Luis Obispo de Tolosa
La Purísima Concepción
Santa Inés
Santa Bárbara
San Buenaventura
San Fernando Rey de España
San Gabriel Arcángel
San Juan Capistrano
San Luis Rey de Francia
San Diego de Alcalá

6

mission to spread their religion. They believed that Catholicism was the one true religion. They wanted to "save" people who were not Catholic, by converting them to Catholicism. The missionaries believed Catholicism would save the American Indians' souls.

Fray Junípero Serra.

The Governor of Baja California, an army captain named Don Gaspar de Portolá, led the soldiers who accompanied the missionaries. The soldiers built presidios, or forts, in Alta California. They protected the land from other countries and protected the missionaries from harm.

Some Christian Indians (Indians who had been converted to Catholicism) from the Baja California missions accompanied the missionaries also. They were from the Baja California missions and wanted to help build the new missions.

In spring of 1769, the missionaries, soldiers, and Christian Indians traveled to Alta California. Some traveled by ship. Fray Serra traveled by land. Their destination was a harbor, discovered 160 years before by early Spanish explorers.

Fray Serra arrived to find that many members of the group who had traveled by ship had become ill. A large number had died. Yet, on July 16th, 1769, Fray Serra founded the first of the Alta California missions

near the harbor and named it San Diego de Alcalá.

Gaspar de Portolá had orders to claim another port, farther north. The early Spanish explorers had named it Monterey, after their viceroy. Portolá's party walked up the coast to find Monterey. In places where cliffs met the sea, they traveled inland through canyons. One time, the group camped by a river. There were several earthquakes while they stayed there, so they named the river Rio San Gabriel de Los Temblores (River of Earthquakes). Near this river, Fray Crespí, a friar in Portolá's party, wrote in his diary, "We came to a valley with a beautiful river. There is a large plain and good land for planting. It is the best place we have seen for a mission." Later, two friars were sent to this spot to found Mission San Gabriel.

Portolá's group went past Monterey but did not recognize it. They continued north and discovered San Francisco Bay. They returned to San Diego. On the trip back, though, they recognized Monterey Bay, but did not stay because they were tired and hungry. There was no food left in San Diego. Most of the American Indians did not want to join the new mission and some were hostile. They did not want the Spaniards to take over their land. Portolá wanted to return to New Spain, but Fray Serra was determined to build the missions.

When a supply ship arrived from New Spain with more food, Fray Serra left Mission San Diego in the hands of two other priests. He traveled north with Portolá to Monterey to establish the second mission.

◀ *Gaspar de Portolá traveled north to find Monterey.*

California's American Indians

After arriving in San Diego's harbor, some Spaniards went to find drinking water. On their way, they saw a native village consisting of about 40 huts by a stream. Each hut was made of willow branches bent into a dome. The branches were covered with tule, or reeds, to protect them from rain. Families of California Indians worked near the huts. Because the weather was warm, they wore little clothing. The men wore belts of string to store food and tools. The women wore deerskin skirts. Their bodies were decorated with beaded jewelry and brightly colored paint.

The Spaniards were impressed by the California Indians' work methods and thought they would make good workers for the missions. Many reported in their diaries that they found the American Indians to be "of good disposition," "well-built," "diligent," and "skillful."

The California Indians knew how to survive by living off the land. Their ancestors had lived in California for over 10,000 years. The women gathered berries, mushrooms, seeds, oats, pine nuts, seaweed, and acorns to eat. They ground the acorn seeds into a mush and cooked it. The men hunted birds and small animals with bows and arrows, sticks and traps. They made canoes and caught fish in the rivers and streams.

Fray Pedro Font, a friar, noted in his diary in 1776, "The Indians are great fishermen and very ingenious. They make baskets of various shapes, and other things very well formed, such as wooden trays and boxes and things made of stone."

The California Indians used their skills to help the Spaniards. The Spaniards depended on supply ships to bring them food. When the ships were late, the Spaniards went hungry. Many times, the California Indians gave them food.

The California Indians made canoes ▶
that were strong and lightweight.

The California Indians' Lifestyle

The California Indians were thankful to the land for giving them what they needed to live. They believed that they had been created from the land. They gave many thanks to their creator. During religious rituals and ceremonies, the California Indians played carved flutes and rattles. They danced and sang songs.

Another ritual for Indian men was to visit *temescals*, or sweat lodges. These were mud huts built near rivers or streams. The men sat inside by a hot fire until they dripped with sweat. Then they jumped into the cold river to cleanse their bodies.

The Indians bathed daily in nearby waterways. In the winter, they kept warm with blankets and capes they'd made from feathers, rabbit fur, or sea otter skins.

The California Indians near Mission San Gabriel belonged to two groups, the Chumash and the

▲
The Chumash Indians built their villages near water.

Tongva. There were many villages, each ruled by a group of elders. The Tongva leaders could be men or women and were called *wots*. Each village also had a shaman, who was a religious leader and a healer. The villagers made the supplies they needed. Some Tongva carved bowls, pipes, and beads from a soft rock called steatite (soapstone). Different villages traded with each other. Most native Californians used beaded shells as money. When food was hard to find, the village leaders got together to divide the food so everyone had enough. Village children learned by watching their elders and listening to stories. The California Indians led a peaceful life.

The Spanish Arrival

When the Spaniards came in big, fancy ships, the American Indians were curious. The Spaniards wore much clothing, spoke a strange language, and gave them beads and shiny gifts.

The missionaries needed the American Indians to join the missions. They needed them to build buildings, plant crops, and live on the missions that were to become Spanish *pueblos*. The missionaries hoped the American Indians would like life on the missions. They would learn Catholicism and many new skills, and become Spanish citizens. The American Indians did not understand the reason behind the missionaries' friendly behavior. They did not know then that they would have to give up their land, their religion, and their old way of life in return.

The Founding Fathers

Fray Serra

Born on a Spanish island called Majorca, Jose Serra had always wanted to be a missionary. He studied hard in school. When he was 17, he became a Franciscan friar. As part of a Franciscan tradition, when he became a friar he changed his name to Junípero, a name which means Juniper, and was given to many Franciscans. Junípero Serra dreamed of going to the New World. He was told that many American Indians lived there. He wanted to teach them Catholicism.

In 1749, Junípero Serra went to the new world of the Americas. After a long, dangerous journey, he arrived in Mexico City, the capital city of New Spain. He attended San Fernando College, a college for Franciscan friars who wanted to be missionaries.

Soon afterwards, Fray Serra volunteered to help with the missions in New Spain. He learned the Indians' language, so he could teach them. Fray Serra was an excellent teacher and a strong preacher. He became president of the Sierra Gorda Missions in New Spain. Then he became president of the Baja California missions.

Although he was 56 and walked with a painful limp, when the chance came to go to Alta California, Fray Serra decided to go. Dressed in a wool robe, wide felt hat, and thick sandals, he walked many miles along California's coasts. During the time between 1769 and his death in 1784, he established the first nine missions in Alta California.

Fray Serra was the father president, or *padre presidente*, of the California missions. He put two friars in charge of each mission. The friars who founded, or began, each mission were the mission's "founding fathers." To help them accomplish this difficult task, they

Fray Serra wearing the traditional clothes of a Franciscan. ▶

14

were given a thick book of rules. The book included everything Spain had learned from establishing its earlier missions. It told the friars how to get the native population to join the mission, the daily schedule to follow, and details like what color clothing the American Indians should wear. Because all the friars used the same rule book, we find many similarities among the 21 California missions.

Other Important Missionaries

When it was time to establish the fourth mission, Fray Serra appointed Fray Angel Fernandez de Somera and Fray Pedro Benito Cambon to be its founding fathers. On September 8th, 1771, Frays Cambon and Somera founded the fourth mission and named it San Gabriel Arcángel, after Saint (San means Saint) Gabriel, God's messenger angel.

Frays Cambon and Somera both fell ill in 1772 due to the hardships of mission life. They retired and Frays Antonio Paterna and Antonio Cruzado took charge of Mission San Gabriel. Fray Cruzado had worked for 22 years in the missions of New Spain. He knew a great deal about agriculture. He served Mission San Gabriel for 32 years and designed its fortress-style church. Fray Paterna had worked 20 years in New Spain's missions. He served Mission San Gabriel for four years until he was called to help found another mission.

There are many respected friars in this mission's history. Fray Miguel Sanchez, a Spanish-born Franciscan friar, served Mission San Gabriel from 1775 to 1803, a total of 28 years. Fray Jose M. de Zalvidea worked tirelessly for the mission from 1806 to 1827. He was known as a strong leader. All these friars, and many others, worked hard to help Mission San Gabriel grow. Under their direction, Mission San Gabriel produced such bountiful harvests and large herds of cattle, it became known as the "Queen of the Missions."

The friars who came to the California missions left their homes and families for a life of hardship.

Founding Mission San Gabriel

In 1771, Frays Cambon and Somera and their team of Baja California Indians and soldiers traveled to Rio San Gabriel de Los Temblores. They founded the fourth mission on the site Crespí and Portolá had discovered.

There is a famous legend about the founding of Mission San Gabriel. As the story goes, when the Spaniards neared the river, Tongva Indians who were angry about the Spanish invasion of Alta California came armed with bows and arrows. Quickly, one of the friars unrolled a picture of the Catholic religious figure, Our Lady of Sorrows, or the Virgin Mary. He showed it to the Indians. The Indians were awestruck. They dropped their weapons. The chiefs placed their necklaces on the ground by the painting. The others followed. The missionaries thought this was a sign of respect for Catholicism. Now, some historians think that the picture of Our Lady of Sorrows, the Virgin Mary, reminded the Tongva Indians of a female spirit they honored called Chukit.

Due to earlier flooding, Cambon and Somera decided the site by the river was not right for the mission. With the Indians, they explored until they found another site, in the San Miguel Valley. There were fertile lands for crops, a river, good timber, and many Indian villages nearby.

Ceremony and Construction

On a hill near a stream in the San Miguel Valley, the friars raised a large cross. They would build the mission here. The American Indians, still fascinated by the missionaries, were willing helpers. They helped the friars build a shelter of branches over an altar. The friars blessed water

It is said that a similar picture of Our Lady of Sorrows saved the missionaries from attack. ▶

from the river and sprinkled it over the cross. They sang Mass, gave a sermon, and rang the new mission bells. The soldiers fired their muskets, and the founding ceremony of San Gabriel Arcángel was complete.

The next day, they began to build. Making walls from willow poles and roofs from tule, they built a chapel, huts for the friars and the soldiers, and corrals for the animals they had brought. The friars, the soldiers, and the Indians worked hard. Within a few days, temporary buildings were finished. The soldiers surrounded the buildings with sharp poles, in case of attack.

San Gabriel's founding fathers knew their work had just begun. The mission had to grow its own food and produce everything it needed to survive. The friars had to convince the American Indians to join the mission. The missionaries set about getting the Indians to join the mission by visiting their villages. They told parents of sick babies that baptizing their children would save the children's souls if the babies were to die. If the baptized children survived, they became part of the mission. When that happened, the parents usually joined the mission, too, to be with their children.

The friars did many things to entice Indians to join the mission. They invited them to

The friars enticed the Chumash and Tongva by showing them shiny religious ornaments like this crucifix.

visit the mission. They showed off shiny religious ornaments and Catholic rituals and music unlike anything the Indians had ever seen. They served the Indians Spanish food. In fact, many American Indians joined the mission because they liked the food served there.

Many American Indians also visited Mission San Gabriel because of Fray Cambon and Fray Somera's friendliness. The friars were glad to have the visitors. However, the large number of Indians also made the friars nervous. They remembered the Tongva Indians who had threatened them before the mission's founding.

Conflict

To maintain control of the American Indians, Fray Somera sent for more soldiers. Unfortunately, many soldiers did not respect the Indians. They saw the Indians as uncivilized. One soldier rode his horse into a nearby village and attacked the wife of a Tongva leader. When the leader found out about the attack, he and his tribe went to the mission to shoot the soldier with arrows. The soldier shot the leader with his musket, then beheaded him and stuck his head on a pole as a warning to other Indians. A few days later, the villagers asked for the head so they could mourn their leader.

After this incident, the Indian villagers stayed far from the mission. San Gabriel's growth was slow. Frays Cambon and Somera became discouraged and fell ill. Frays Paterna and Cruzado, two other missionaries in Alta California, stopped at Mission San Gabriel on their way to found Mission San Buenaventura. They saw the trouble and stayed there, allowing Frays Cambon and Somera to retire and leave the mission.

Frays Paterna and Cruzado worked hard to regain the Indians' trust and keep the soldiers in line. They were gentle and patient. The Indians began offering their children for baptism. Surprisingly, one of the first children to be baptized was the son of the slain Indian leader. He was offered for baptism by his mother.

Joining the Mission

California Indians who joined the mission were called neophytes. A neophyte is a person who has just joined the Christian Church. Adult neophytes were given two years of instruction in Catholicism and then baptized. Neophytes were given clothing to wear and lived in huts on or near the mission. The missionaries kept careful records of how many neophytes joined the mission. They believed that each new neophyte was a soul saved.

Once they joined the mission, the neophytes were not allowed to leave. At older missions the Spaniards discovered that if the neophytes could leave the missions, many ran away. They forgot what they had learned, lost their clothing, and returned to their old ways. The friars believed the missions taught the Indians a better, more civilized, way of life.

At the mission, the neophytes had little chance to practice their old religion, see their families, or go to the places they loved. They were forced to follow the mission's strict schedule, which included prayers, lessons, and work. The neophytes became homesick. The friars gave the neophytes a two-week vacation every five weeks to return to their villages.

The Indians were baptized when they were accepted into the Christian faith. ▶

MISSION SAN GABRIEL ARCÁNGEL

CEMETERY

COCINA

MODERN
CHAPEL

BAPTISTRY

PULPIT

JACRISTY

ADOBE WALLS
STONE WALLS

Building The Mission

The friars and neophytes at Mission San Gabriel worked hard to raise cattle and plant fields. However, spring floods from the nearby river destroyed their crops. Four years after Mission San Gabriel was founded, it was moved. The friars, soldiers, and about 150 neophytes moved the mission farther north in the valley.

They built new buildings from branches and tule. These were temporary buildings. After new fields were planted and other work was finished, it was time to plan permanent buildings.

The Mission Structure

The friars looked in their book of rules. Like all Spanish missions, Mission San Gabriel was to be built in a quadrangle, around a courtyard. In one corner would be the church. Next to it would be the *convento*, with the friars' bedrooms and guest quarters. There would be soldiers' rooms, a kitchen, workshops, a granary to store grain, and dormitories, called *monjerío*, for the neophytes. Girls and unmarried women would live in the *monjerío*. Married neophyte families would live in huts. There would be only one gate to the mission so soldiers could protect it from attack and keep the neophytes from leaving.

Now construction began. The mission had few supplies. The one thing they had a lot of was a clay-like dirt, called adobe. Under the direction of the friars, and with the help of the Christian Indians from Baja California, the neophytes learned to use this adobe to make bricks. They mixed the adobe with water to make mud and threw in some straw and crushed grass. The neophytes stomped in the adobe to mix it. Then it was molded into bricks and set in the sun to dry.

◀ *This map shows the layout of Mission San Gabriel.*

A neophyte boy guarded the bricks from wandering animals.

The bricks were constructed into walls, 6 to 10 feet thick. They had to stand up against earthquakes and support heavy roofs. Roofs were made, as before, from poles and tule.

Although the adobe bricks were strong, there was a problem. When it rained, the adobe fell apart. To fix the problem, the neophytes covered the bricks with a waterproof white plaster they were taught to make with crushed limestone and sand. They added eaves, or overhanging edges, to the roofs to protect the walls from rain. The corridors connecting the buildings were also given roofs. Later, the people at the San Antonio mission learned to make red

This man is making adobe bricks. Once they are molded, he leaves them in the sun to dry.

Spanish roof tiles, called *tejas*, and San Gabriel soon followed. By 1790, most of California's mission buildings had red tiled roofs.

Whitewashed adobe, wide overhanging eaves, and covered corridors are now known as mission-style architecture. Buildings of this style are still seen today in California and other places where Spanish missions were built.

In 1790, the friars asked the government to send artisans, or craftsmen, from Mexico to help build the mission buildings. When the stonemasons, blacksmiths, and carpenters arrived at the missions, they helped build stone fountains, pillars, arches, ironwork, and bell towers.

Growth at Mission San Gabriel Arcángel

Mission San Gabriel had been growing steadily since Frays Cruzado and Paterna took over. Now it had the second largest number of neophytes of all the California missions. Mission San Gabriel needed a bigger church. When Fray Cruzado designed the new church, he was probably thinking of the famous cathedral of Cordova, Spain, which he had seen as a child. That cathedral was originally a mosque built by the Moors. The Moors were Muslims from Africa who conquered much of Spain in the middle ages. Their buildings influenced many features of Spanish architecture.

The artisans and neophytes of Mission San Gabriel built the bottom half of the new church with stone and concrete. From the windows up, brick was used. In the Moorish style, they built long, narrow windows. Between each window, they built buttresses, or support columns, with pyramid caps. They also built arched doorways, like the Moors. The

27

The missionaries at Mission San Gabriel wanted their church to be in the Moorish style, like the one shown here.

church's vaulted roof was replaced by a flat roof after an earthquake. The finished church looked strong and solid, like a fortress. It's architecture is called fortress-style.

The friars wanted the neophytes to feel good about their church. They sent for brushes and "how to paint" books. The neophytes chose rich colors, such as forest green and deep red to paint and decorate the inside of the church. Colored rocks were crushed and mixed with olive oil to make paint.

In 1805, after 14 years of work, the church was finished.

Unfortunately, the elderly Frays Cruzado and Paterna died that year. They were both buried within the sanctuary. San Gabriel's church is considered the best example of fortress-style architecture in a mission church.

To the right of the church entrance, a bell tower was built. The adobe wall had arched holes in which the mission's bells were hung. The largest bell, called the angelus bell, weighed over a ton. In 1812, an earthquake toppled the belltower. It was rebuilt as a *campanario*,

The bells in the campanario *called the neophytes to work.*

or bell wall, at the end of the church's long side wall. Bell ringers climbed an outdoor stone staircase and crossed the loft where the choir sang to get to the belfry.

In the 1820s, four mills were built to grind flour, make olive oil, and saw wood. Two of the mills were powered by mules. The other two, a sawmill and one gristmill, were water-powered.

A Day on Mission San Gabriel

Each day at Mission San Gabriel, the neophytes awoke at sunrise to the ringing of bells. Soon afterwards, the large angelus bell called them to church. The friars led an hour of prayers. Another bell announced breakfast, which was *atole*, a hot cereal made of ground, roasted grain.

Work on the Mission

When the bell rang again it was time to work. Even children had jobs. The friars and Baja California neophytes taught every neophyte at the mission a job. Many neophyte men were taught farming. In the fields, they grew corn, wheat, barley, lentils, garbanzo beans, and cotton. In the gardens, they grew onions, garlic, tomatoes, chile, and melons. There were orchards, too, with orange trees, citrons, limes, apples, pears, peaches, pomegranates, figs, and olives. In 1834, San Gabriel reported having 2,333 fruit trees. The mission even grew fences! A 12-foot tall cactus hedge was grown to fence in cattle. One year, the hedge bore over 37,000 bushels of prickly pear fruit! San Gabriel also had a 170-acre vineyard. The mission became famous for producing fine wines.

The neophytes plowed, planted, and built aqueducts to irrigate the fields. Boys guarded the fields from livestock. After harvest, the neophytes threshed the wheat and then ground it into flour.

Many women and girls did their work in the *monjerío*. A *llavera*, meaning keeper of the keys, supervised their work and held the keys to the *monjerío*. The *llavera* was usually a soldier's wife. She taught the ladies to spin yarn, sew, and weave. They made ponchos for the shepherds, habits for the friars, clothing, and blankets.

This is a grapevine in the Mission ▶
San Gabriel vineyard.

Neophyte women made baskets and bowls.

The *llavera* also supervised cooking. The neophyte women fixed *atole* in the kitchen for breakfast and dinner, and cooked lunch in kettles over a fire outside.

Lunch was *pozole*, a meat stew with beans, corn, and vegetables, served with tortillas or *atole*. After lunch was rest time, or *siesta*, from 2:00 to 4:00 PM. Then, the bell rang and work resumed.

Many neophyte men worked on *ranchos*, which were farms where the mission's herds were raised. As the mission's gardens and fields took up more room, *ranchos* were established surrounding the mission. San Gabriel had about 15 *ranchos*. Its most well-known cattle ranch was called San Bernardino.

A *mayordomo*, who was a baptized Indian from New Spain, supervised work on the *ranchos*. Neophytes who worked on the *ranchos* herded cattle, milked cows, fed pigs, sheared sheep, groomed horses, and guarded the oxen. The neophytes branded San Gabriel's cattle with a "T" for *temblores*, or earthquake.

During La Matanza, the slaughtering season, cattle were killed and hides were stretched out to dry. The mission wasted nothing. Sheep skin was used for parchment. Meat was eaten, and shared with the soldiers at the presidios. Rawhide was used to hang bells and doors. Sometimes the door itself was made from rawhide. Rawhide could also be scraped and oiled and used as a window. Tanned hides were made into saddles, shoes, and the leather jackets worn by soldiers. Sometimes neophytes used hides to trade for other supplies.

The fat from cattle was boiled down into tallow, which was used for soap and candles. Neophyte girls helped dip many candles needed to light the mission's rooms at night. Other neophytes prepared sheep's wool for weaving. Children removed burs and sticks from the wool. Then it was washed, dried, carded, straightened, and spun into yarn.

Mission San Gabriel's workshops were busy. An American trapper named Harrison Rogers stayed at the mission in 1826. He wrote in his diary, "I walked through the workshops. I saw some Indians blacksmithing, some carpentering, others making the woodwork of ploughs, others employed in making spinning wheels for the squaws (women) to spin on. There is upwards of sixty women employed in spinning yarn and others weaving."

The neophytes made wine and olive oil, cheese and butter. Men learned metal working, carpentry, farming, masonry, tanning, and herding. Women learned to spin wool, weave, sew, cook, and make candles and soap.

A Mission Education

The neophytes were given a formal education, too. The children had lessons each morning and afternoon. At first the friars tried to teach

Catholicism in the neophytes' language. However, their language did not have words to fit the foreign religion. Also, neophytes from different villages spoke different versions of the language.

THIS IS ONE COMPLETE BIBLE IN SIX VOLUMES BOUND IN SHEEP-SKIN (VELLUM), PRINTED IN THE YEAR 1588, VENICE, ITALY. IT IS UNIQUE NOT ONLY FROM THE STAND-POINT OF COPIOUS EXPLANATORY NOTES, BUT OF THE NUMEROUS AND CAREFULLY DRAFTED ILLUSTRATIONS. THESE VOLUMES WERE A PRIZED POSSESSION OF THE ORIGINAL LIBRARY WHICH ONCE INCLUDED HUNDREDS OF VOLUMES.

◀ *The neophytes at the mission learned about Catholicism and the Bible.*

◀ *The friars taught the neophytes Catholic songs and blessings.*

The friars taught the neophytes Spanish. They taught songs, prayers, and blessings. A group of boys were chosen for a choir. They learned to read, write, sing, and play instruments. During special events they performed for the mission.

Nighttime at the Mission

At 5:00 PM the angelus bell rang for prayers. Supper, at 6:00 PM, was *atole* and maybe some mission wine. After dinner there was free time. The neophytes could rest, play games, or visit with each other on the mission. At 8:00 PM the bell rang one last time, calling the neophytes back to their quarters for bed.

The friars sometimes gave the neophytes breaks from the daily routine. Sabbath was observed on Sunday with morning Mass and lots of free time. The neophytes raced horses, played games and gambled.

Holy days and festivals, such as the harvest celebration, were an important part of mission life. Festivals featured huge feasts, bull fights, concerts, Indian dances, firecrackers, and games, all accompanied by the ringing of the mission bells.

The mission bells rang to signal events over the course of the day.

Hardship on the Mission

There was joy at Mission San Gabriel, but there was also much suffering. For everyone at the mission, there were hardships.

Many of the friars disliked managing the activities of the mission. They were not trained to be farmers and builders. They were trained to be priests. Managing the mission was an enormous job.

Everyone on the mission endured nature's bad temper. In 1812, San Gabriel was hit by a large earthquake. The church was badly damaged. The bell tower, the friars' rooms, and many workshops were destroyed. It took years of work to repair the damage and build a new *campanario*. The friars moved into the granary, which they converted to a church.

A Hard Life for the Mission Indians

The neophytes on the mission suffered the most hardship of all. Mission life was not like life in the villages, where they were free to follow their own customs. On the mission, the neophytes had to wear different clothing, eat different foods, practice a different religion, and do different work. For example, men were used to resting for long periods between hunts. Now they had to follow the strict routine of the mission. The friars appointed a few neophytes as officers, called *alcaldes*, to supervise work in the mission fields and workshops. *Alcaldes* carried rods or whips to remind the workers to work hard in order to avoid punishment. The neophytes had to make food and supplies not only for the mission, but for the nearby presidios, too.

Neophytes could not change their minds and decide to leave the mission. Runaways were hunted down by soldiers, returned to the mission, and sometimes whipped. Although they knew they would be

The neophytes had to work hard at the mission. ▶

punished, many neophytes still tried to escape from the mission.

In their villages, the California Indians were free to live together with their families. At the mission, families were unable to live together. Unmarried women and neophyte girls over 13 years old had to live inside a locked *monjerío*. They slept, ate, and sometimes worked there, too. It was Spanish custom for daughters to sleep in locked or guarded rooms. The friars felt it was their job to protect the women from attack by soldiers or other men at the mission by keeping them locked in at night.

In the *monjeríos*, the women neophytes lived in small rooms, very close together. Because so many people lived in these tiny rooms, the *monjerío* quickly became dirty and smelly. Disease spread quickly among the girls and women because of the unclean living conditions.

Sickness and Death

There was much sickness throughout Mission San Gabriel. The friars, soldiers, and visitors unknowingly brought germs with them from New Spain. The neophytes had never been exposed to these germs before, so their bodies were unable to fight them. Diseases like smallpox, cholera, and dysentery spread quickly among the neophytes.

The friars tried to heal the sick. They separated sick neophytes from the rest to stop diseases from spreading. However, there was little they could do. In a report to the Spanish Government dated 1814, San Gabriel's friars wrote that the number of deaths at the mission was double the number of births. They said, of the neophytes who were born, three out of four died before age two and very few survived to reach adulthood. Frays Zalvidea and Taboada, two other missionaries in Alta

California pleaded in the report, "If the government does not supply doctors and medicine, Upper California will be without any Indians at all." That year, Fray Zalvidea had a hospital built near the mission. The hospital was nearly always full.

▲

Many California Indians died of European diseases like smallpox.

In 1825, an epidemic of smallpox and cholera spread through Mission San Gabriel. It is estimated that three of every four neophytes died.

Altogether, nearly 6,000 Indians are buried in the mission's cemetery, more than at any of California's other missions.

The natives living near the mission heard about the suffering. They saw the mission fields and pastures take over land they had once used for hunting and gathering food. They saw much of their culture and heritage slipping away.

The Rise of the *Pueblos*
and the Fall of the Missions

The *Pueblos*

Since Mission San Gabriel sat along three important trails, many settlers stopped there during their travels. The friars became tired of visitors. Many caused trouble. Despite the protests of the missionaries, the Spanish governor of California, Governor de Neve, decided to establish a *pueblo*, or town, near the mission. The visitors could stay at the *pueblo*.

In December 1781, the Spanish government founded the new *pueblo* and San Gabriel's friars blessed it. It was named Nuestra Señora de los Angeles del Rio de Porciuncula, meaning Our Lady of the Angels by the River of Portincula. Later, the town shortened its name to Los Angeles.

The government asked the missions, as the most established settlements in California, to help build new *pueblos*. Mission San Gabriel gave each of Los Angeles' settlers horses, farm animals, cattle, and branding irons. The government supplied them with the means to buy food until crops were harvested.

The Growth of Los Angeles

Los Angeles grew quickly. In 1788, they chose their first mayor, a Mexican Indian named Jose Vanegas. Within 10 years, Los Angeles had 29 adobe houses, a town hall, granaries, barracks, and a guardhouse, all surrounded by an adobe wall. It had a population of 139 people. The settlers of Los Angeles produced more grain than any mission except San Gabriel. Perhaps the reason for this was that the settlers hired the well-trained neophytes of Mission San Gabriel to work their fields. The friars allowed some of the mission's neophytes to work for pay at the *pueblo*.

This church was built near the mission. ▶

Mission San Gabriel's friars often had to travel the nine long miles to the *pueblo* to help the settlers. The friars urged the settlers of Los Angeles to establish their own church. However, it was not until 1814 that the building of the church began. Finally, in 1822, with much help from San Gabriel and other missions, a church was established in Los Angeles. It was named Our Lady of the Angels, and still stands today. Los Angeles continued to grow and, from 1835 until 1849, it was the capital of California.

In the early 1800s, as Los Angeles grew, its settlers became frustrated with Mission San Gabriel. The settlers needed land for their herds and farms, but all the nearby land belonged to Mission San Gabriel and Mission San Fernando Rey de España. The missions had California's best land. The settlers of California complained.

Secularization

The Spanish government listened to the settlers. Perhaps it was time to secularize California's missions and turn them into *pueblos*. (To secularize means to make the missions non-religious.) This was the final part of King Carlos III's plan to claim Alta California for Spain. The neophytes would become Spanish citizens. The mission land would be given to the neophytes, and the mission would operate as a Spanish *pueblo*.

The government asked the friars if the neophytes had become good Catholics, learned Spanish ways, and mastered the skills necessary to run the missions. The friars said no. They felt that the neophytes still needed guidance to do their work.

However, the government and California's settlers wanted ownership of California's land. Also, many felt that the neophytes should be free.

The Spanish government passed laws to free the neophytes, but the neophytes were not freed. The Spanish government and soldiers were too busy to enforce the laws. New Spain had begun a war with Spain to free itself from the rule of Spain's government. In 1822, New Spain won its independence and became the country of Mexico. Now the California missions were governed by Mexico.

There were more attempts to secularize the missions. In 1826, a law freed all neophytes who had been Christians for over 15 years. Some neophytes gladly left the missions. Others did not want to leave the friars. Mission life was the only life they knew. Still other neophytes, who were not yet free, became discontent.

On August 17, 1833, the Mexican government passed its final law secularizing the missions of upper and lower California. The missions would be called *pueblos*. Government administrators would supervise them.

▲
Life became harder for many neophytes after secularization.

Disappointment for the American Indians

Much of the mission land was taken over by the settlers and the government, although it had been promised to the neophytes. A few neophytes were given mission land. However, many did not want to

43

herd and farm anymore. They returned to their old villages, only to find that the land had been taken by settlers. A large number of neophytes went to work at *pueblos* or *ranchos*. They used their skills to help the settlers. Other neophytes rebelled against the missions by gambling away their mission clothing and land. Some settlers used trickery and robbery to get the neophytes' land. Most neophytes lost all they had.

An administrator, Colonel Nicolas Gutierrez, took over the new *pueblo* of San Gabriel. Mission San Gabriel's two friars, Frays Ibarra and Estenga, continued to lead services at San Gabriel's church. The administrator took charge of all other mission activities. The friars couldn't stand to see the mission falling apart under the careless leadership of the administrator. They felt unable to help the neophytes who remained. In 1835, they fled the church. They asked the *padre presidente*, or president of the missions, to forgive them for leaving their posts. Other friars came to San Gabriel's church to care for the neophytes.

In 1842, the Mexican government panicked. The missions were not producing enough food or supplies for the presidios. San Gabriel and 11 other missions were returned to the friars. When Fray Estenga returned to San Gabriel, almost everything was gone. Almost all of the 16,500 cattle had been killed for their hides. Less than 100 remained. Most mission land was in the hands of strangers. The workshops and pantries were empty. The only neophytes left were the sick, the old, and some orphaned children.

In 1845, the settlers of California, called Californios, rebelled against the Mexican government. The Mexican governor surrendered and the Californios elected their own governor, Pio Pico. Pico had been born at Mission San Gabriel, the son of a soldier. In 1846, Governor Pico sold

Mission San Gabriel to American settlers to pay a debt. Henry Dalton, caretaker of the mission before the sale, wrote to Governor Pico on February 4, 1846, "May it please you to bring in the knowledge that the property is in complete ruin."

Statehood for California

In the summer of 1846, the United States sent troops, both by ship and overland, to occupy California. The United States wanted ownership of California. When the U.S. troops occupied Los Angeles, California's capital, the Californios surrendered. The Treaty of Cahuenga was signed on January 13, 1847, giving the United States control of California.

In 1850, California became the 31st state. President Buchanan gave the mission property back to the Catholic church in 1859. Catholic friars revived San Gabriel's deserted church and made it a parish church. People began to take an interest in the missions as a part of California's history. Efforts were made to restore Mission San Gabriel. In 1886, the windows of the church were enlarged and the inside walls were plastered.

President Buchanan returned the missions to the Catholic church.

In 1908, the Claretian religious order, members of the Roman Catholic group, The Missionary Sons of the Immaculate Heart of Mary, took over Mission San Gabriel. They continue to operate San Gabriel's church as a parish church for the Bishop of Monterey.

Mission San Gabriel Today

Today, the huge city of Los Angeles surrounds Mission San Gabriel. Many visitors come to see San Gabriel's fortress-style church, and its museum, buildings, gardens, and *campanario*.

For nine years, the mission's bells were silent. The *campanario* was damaged in a 1987 earthquake. Yet another earthquake struck in 1994. After this, the United States federal government helped to restore the *campanario*. In 1996, on its 225th anniversary, Mission San Gabriel's six bells rang again. Years ago, settlers claimed they could hear the mission's angelus bell ringing from the *pueblo* of Los Angeles, nine miles away. Today, the bells still ring out over the din of the passing traffic and rumbling trains.

When you step inside the mission, just past the monument of Fray Serra, you will find many clues about its past. The inside of the church still glows with the colors painted by the neophytes: deep red, gold, and forest green. The altar holds six carved wooden statues brought from Spain in 1791. The statue in the center is of Saint Gabriel. The original pulpit where the friars stood long ago and prayed with the neophytes still stands. People still pray in San Gabriel's church. Two services are held there each Sunday.

▲

This statue of Fray Serra stands at the entrance of the mission.

Today many visitors come to Mission San Gabriel Arcángel. ▶

FATHER
JVNIPERO SERRA

ONE HVNDRED
AND FIFTIETH
ANNIVERSARY
SAN GABRIEL
MISSION
1771-1921

On a wall hangs the 300-year-old painting of Our Lady of Sorrows, famous from the legend of the mission's founding. The museum displays the oldest known paintings by neophytes, a series of paintings of the Stations of the Cross (part of the Catholic religious beliefs).

A painting of Our Lady of Sorrows.

Hints of the Past

While most of the mission buildings and workshops fell to ruins long ago, there are still hints of their past. Many of the foundations still remain. The winery, the oldest and once the largest in California, has just been restored. Visitors can see the original kitchen and the open fireplace where neophytes prepared meals. The brick tanks of the tannery are there, and there are also four deep brick-lined holes in the ground that were part of the soap and tallow factory. Carved into the bottom of one of the mission's wooden doors is a cat door! One of the first things San Gabriel's friars requested from New Spain were two cats. The mission had mice!

Visitors can see the small quarters where the friars slept. They can follow a pathway to the gardens. The corridor is shaded by three grape arbors with vines from the original vineyard. The first grapevine,

This pathway is kept cool by the shade from the grapevine.

planted in 1826, is still growing, too. It has gotten so thick that it has cracked the pavement that surrounds it. The beautiful courtyard shows off a stone fountain and an anchor from an old Spanish supply ship. There are also replicas of all 21 missions built by Claretian seminary students in 1932. Outside the church wall are the bricks of the original bell tower built in 1775.

Just outside the church is Mission San Gabriel's Indian cemetery, the oldest cemetery in Los Angeles county. There lie 6,000 American Indians, whose lives built Mission San Gabriel. Some of the worshipers

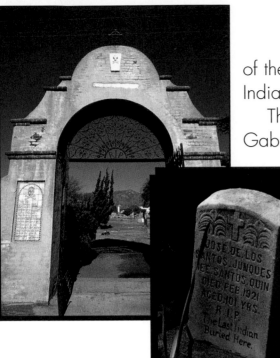

of the church today are descendants of the Indians buried here.

The road leading from Mission San Gabriel began as a small trail connecting California's 21 missions. Now, that trail is a well-traveled highway, called the King's Highway, or El Camino Real. It winds up and down California's coastline, reminding us of those who traveled before us.

In the 64 years between Fray Serra's founding of the first mission in 1769 and secularization in 1833, the Spanish missions changed the face and fabric of California.

Many California Indians died as a result of European colonization.

The introduction of herding and farming changed California's landscape. Vineyards and orange trees, brought by the Spaniards, remain important crops in California today. Examples of mission-style architecture, such as whitewashed adobe buildings with red tiled roofs, are seen throughout California. Many California cities, like Los Angeles, proudly bear Spanish names.

California's people were changed, too. Tragically, much of the rich heritage and culture of the California Indians was crowded out by the missions. In its place came Catholicism, the Spanish language, and a

Today Mission San Gabriel Arcángel stands as a monument to the complex history of California.

European way of life. The Spanish missions have done much in making California what it is today.

Make Your Own
Mission San Gabriel Arcángel

To make your own model of the San Gabriel Arcángel mission, you will need:

foamcore board
Styrofoam
red construction paper
glue
beige and green paint
toothpicks

two miniature bells
ruler
X-Acto knife (ask for adult's help)

Directions

Step 1: Cut out a piece of foamcore that is 20" by 20" for the mission base. Paint the base green.

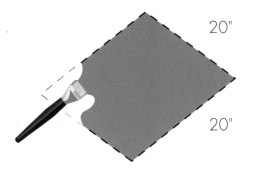

20"

20"

Adult supervision is suggested.

Step 2: Cut 2 pieces of Styrofoam that are 9″ by 9″ to make the front and back of the church. Cut out a window and front door on one piece.

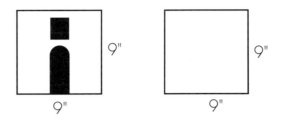

Step 3: Cut out a piece of Styrofoam that is 8″ by 9″. This will be the left side of the church. Paint all 3 walls beige.

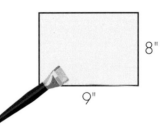

Step 4: Position the church walls on the base to form 3 sides of a box. Glue the pieces in place and let dry.

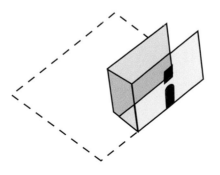

Step 5: Cut out 3 pieces of Styrofoam that are 4″ by 20″ and one piece that is 4″ by 11″.

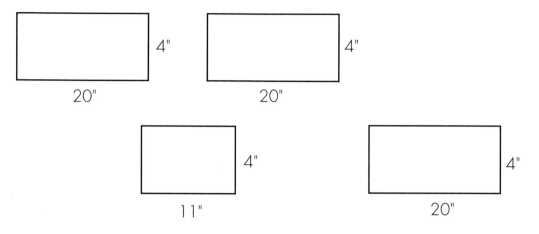

Step 6: Paint all 4 pieces beige. Glue them to the base around the edges so that they form the courtyard walls.

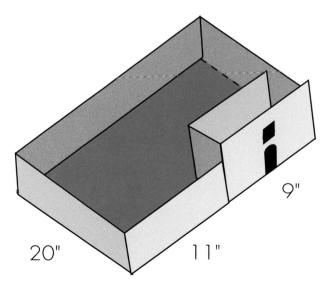

Step 7: Make a main bell tower by cutting a piece of Styrofoam that is 2" by 3". Cut out 2 windows from the bell tower.

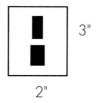

3"

2"

Step 8: Cut out a small half circle whose bottom is 2" and cut out a window from it. Put this piece on top of the bell tower.

2"

Step 9: Place the belltower on the board beside the church. Make 2 more small bell towers for the church by cutting 6 pieces of Styrofoam 0.5" by 1.5".

☐ ☐ ☐ ☐ ☐ ☐

Step 10: Glue a .5″ by 1.5″ Styrofoam piece on top of two other .5″ by 1.5″ pieces as shown below. Repeat with the other 3 foam pieces and attach to the top of the church.

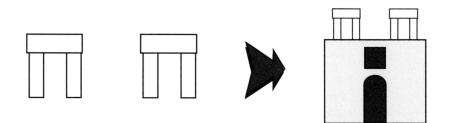

Step 11: Paint all Styrofoam pieces beige. Let dry.

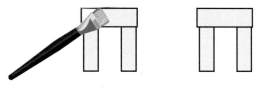

Step 12: Stick a toothpick through the top of a miniature bell and insert the end of the toothpick into the main bell tower. Do this with the other 2 bells and insert into the other bell towers.

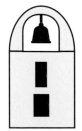

Step 13: Fold a piece of red paper back and forth to make it look rippled. Cut into strips and glue the ends of the paper to the front and back walls so it stretches over the tops of the walls.

Step 14: Bend 2 strips of red paper into a triangle and glue to the small towers. Cut out Styrofoam crosses and insert in the top of the church with toothpicks.

Step 15: Decorate around the mission with greenery and flowers. You can make these decorations with colored tissue paper, or paint them on to the mission directly.

*Use the above mission as a reference for building your mission.

Important Dates in Mission History

1492	Christopher Columbus reaches the West Indies
1542	Cabrillo's expedition to California
1602	Sebastian Vizcaíno sails to California
1713	Fray Junípero Serra is born
1769	Founding of San Diego de Alcalá
1770	Founding of San Carlos Borromeo del Río Carmelo
1771	Founding of San Antonio de Padua and San Gabriel Arcángel
1772	Founding of San Luis Obispo de Tolosa
1775–76	Founding of San Juan Capistrano
1776	Founding of San Francisco de Asís
1776	Declaration of Independence is signed
1777	Founding of Santa Clara de Asís
1782	Founding of San Buenaventura
1784	Fray Serra dies
1786	Founding of Santa Bárbara Virgen y Mártir
1787	Founding of La Purísima Concepción de Maria Santísima
1791	Founding of Santa Cruz and Nuestra Señora de la Soledad
1797	Founding of San José, San Juan Bautista, San Miguel Arcángel, and San Fernando Rey de España
1798	Founding of San Luis Rey de Francia
1804	Founding of Santa Inés Virgen y Mártir
1817	Founding of San Rafael Arcángel
1823	Founding of San Francisco de Solano
1849	Gold found in northern California
1850	California becomes the 31st state

Glossary

adobe (uh-DOH-bee) A clay-like dirt which can be mixed with water, straw, and crushed grass and then dried in the sun to make bricks.

Alta California (AL-tuh kah-lih-FOR-nee-uh) A name meaning upper California that the Spaniards called the land that is now the state of California.

angelus (AN-jel-es) A bell rung at morning, noon, and night to call Catholics to recite a prayer called the Angelus.

Baja California (BAH-hah kah-lih-FOR-nee-uh) A name meaning lower California that the Spaniards called the strip of land off the northwest coast of Mexico.

baptism (BAP-tiz-uhm) Welcoming a person to Christianity by a ceremony that involves covering or sprinkling them with water.

Catholicism (kuh-THAHL-uh-siz-uhm) The religion of the Catholic church.

cholera (KAHL-er-uh) An infectious disease that causes problems in the intestines.

Claretian (kluh-REE-shun) A member of the Roman Catholic group, The Missionary Sons of the Immaculate Heart of Mary, founded in 1849 by Anthony Claret.

dysentery (DIS-en-ter-ee) A disease of the large intestine.

eaves (EEVZ) The lower edges of a roof that stick out over the walls.

Franciscan (fran-SIS-ken) A member of a Roman Catholic group founded by Saint Francis of Assisi in Italy in 1209.

missionary (MIH-shuh-nay-ree) A person who works to spread their religion or way of thinking to other people.

Moors (MOORZ) A group of Muslim people who came from Africa and conquered much of Spain in the Middle Ages.

neophyte (NEE-oh-fyt) Someone who has recently joined the Christian church.

secularize (SEHK-yoo-luh-ryz) Taking control away from the church and its priests and giving it to the government and citizens.

seminary (SEM-in-ehr-ee) A school for training priests.

shaman (SHAH-man) An American Indian religious leader and healer.

smallpox (SMAWL-poks) A very infectious illness, known for fever and pox.

tule (TOO-lee) Reeds used by the Indians to make homes and boats.

viceroy (VYS-roy) A governor who rules and acts as the representative of the king.

Pronunciation Guide

alcaldes (ahl-KAHL-days)

atole (ah-TOH-lay)

campanario (kahm-pahn-AR-ee-oh)

convento (kahn-VEN-toh)

El Camino Real (EL kah-MEE-noh RAY-al)

llavera (yah-VAYR-ah)

mayordomo (may-or-DOH-moh)

monjerío (mohn-HAYR-ee-oh)

padre presidente (PAH-dray preh-SIH-dent-ay)

pozole (poh-ZOH-lay)

pueblo (PWAY-bloh)

ranchos (RAHN-chohz)

siesta (see-EHS-tah)

teja (TAY-hah)

temblores (tem-BLOR-ays)

temescals (TEH-mes-kul)

wots (WAHTS)

Resources

For more information on the California Missions, check out these books, Web sites, and other resources.

Books
MacMillan, Dianne. *Missions of the Los Angeles Area*. Minneapolis, MN: Lerner Publications Company, 1996.
Schwabacher, Martin. *The Chumash Indians*. Mexico: Chelsea House Publishers, 1995.
Van Steenwyk, Elizabeth. *The California Missions*. New York, NY: Franklin Watts, 1995.

Web Sites
http://www.escusd.k12.ca.us/missiontrail.html
http://tqd.advanced.org/3615/mission4.shtml
http://www.rutledge.com/Westridge/Students/missions/home.htm

Videos
Howser, Huell. *California's Gold*, California Missions #102.

Other
Mission San Gabriel Arcangel
537 West Mission Drive
San Gabriel, CA 91776
Museum Phone: 626/457-3048

Index